MW00596464

Language of the Soul

Language of the Soul

Fifty-Two Affirmations to Guide You

Elizabeth Irvine

Published by Truewellbeing

ISBN (hardcover): 978-0-9776178-2-1

A dedication to my father,

My dad was an engineering professor and an authority on ergonomics, the study of humans in their environment. He taught and lived the mantra "work smart." He even had the words transcribed onto his license plate. Now I understand my dad, who knew nothing of affirmations, in fact lived by their essence and unknowingly taught me to understand them.

Like my dad, affirmations are all about *working smart*—saying more with less. The ideas and affirmations in this book are presented briefly and simply. They ask us to cut through the clutter of our lives and focus our minds on one essential truth each day. They ask us to work smart.

Author's Note

To the reader,

To truly know yourself is possibly life's greatest joy. But how do you find out more about yourself—what brings you meaning and happiness and allows a deeply fulfilling life?

I wrote this book over the span of many years with a clear intention: to create a sacred guide book that brings comfort, offers encouragement, and shows a clear path to uncovering your divinity, your soul essence.

Using these short, positive resolutions has taught me to bring awareness to where I am putting my energies—in my thoughts, words, and actions—and to become comfortable and confident with my choices from deep within. In this place I feel whole and happy more often.

Affirmations have led me to a new way of life, an existence that feels more meaningful and holds a sense of ease and grace. My hope is that the book you now hold in your hands will do the same for you.

Introduction

You have the opportunity to take a journey. It will lead you to a place you've probably never been—few of us have. And yet when you get there, you'll find that somehow you know this place. It's familiar to you. It fills you with deep peace, joy, and fulfillment. In this place, you'll speak a different language and have a fresh way of living. Here, you are your best self—your true self. Experiencing this incredible place and a new way of living takes some effort; you'll have to leave the comfort of your daily routine. You are so capable of this journey. You just need a guide.

It's my intention that this book lead you into a new paradigm. To teach you how to use your energetic life force to think and speak differently and to become comfortable and confident with your choices from deep within. This is the place where you will begin to feel more whole and happy more often.

Begin Speaking Soul Language

Speaking soul language is about saying more with less. Affirmations are an important part of soul language. They are short, clear, positive statements that create clarity, form intention, and guide you. An affirmation asks you to cut through the clutter of your life and focus your mind on one essential truth at a time. Your words become your power. You are awakening to your thoughts, behaviors, and emotions—getting to know you a little better.

Over the past twenty-five years I have developed an intimacy with my practice of meditation and affirmation work. These decades of habit have helped me create an energetic vibration at the very center of my daily life.

Affirmation: I use my words as power. I mean what I say and say what I mean.

Imagine This

Right now, imagine the quiet, still space that exists deep within you. Take a few long, deep, soothing breaths—in … and out. Inhale. Exhale. Notice how your breath creates space in your body and between your thoughts. Use your breath to let go of built-up stress, and reconnect—even just briefly—to the deepest part of you that is whole and pure. Bring your awareness deep within to your own uniquely beautiful divine light. In this place you hold the answers.

Now ask the question, "What would I like to change in my life?" You are sending a message from your conscious mind to your subconscious. It is not a wish or a hope but an intention for positive change. Form your intention for change—whatever that may be—into a short positive statement. For example, the desire "I want to have a new career" would become the affirmation "My inner light shines bright, and I attract new opportunities to support me." It is not "I will not accept my current work"; it is "I am a talented soul, and I feel freedom and joy in what I do."

A Force of Energy

The practice of using affirmations involves more than just making declarations. It is supporting your positive statements through your conscious energy. Here's an example: The desired change of wanting to lose ten pounds would become the affirmation "I am healthy and vibrantly alive; I eat only nutritious food." You would then channel the feeling of what it's like to be healthier, be lighter in weight, and have focused energy. Tap into the power of your imagination, and visualize being healthy and feeling vibrantly alive. See yourself choosing a green juice or healthy smoothie for breakfast, instead of a heavier bacon, egg, and cheese croissant. Can you sense the shift—feeling lighter, more satisfied, and happy with your choice? If this is an affirmation that resonates with you, take this choice into action: Choose something healthy for breakfast tomorrow, and physically notice how you feel. Small steps add up.

Soul work must be grounded in action to bring about consistent change. It takes daily commitment and diligence, but soon you'll get the hang of it and come to understand how wonderful this new way of being the best version of yourself feels. Your intentional statement, fueled with feeling, turns into physical action and like a GPS will guide you home.

Affirmation: My actions align with my goals and create my life.

The Shadow, Embracing Wholeness

To work on our light, we also have to journey into the shadow. Affirmations ask us to look at our "shadow" side—which is the opposite of what we want to attract. Let's come back to the example affirmation "My inner light shines bright, and I attract new opportunities to support me." Unknowingly, we can sabotage our affirmation by thinking, *Who am I kidding? I will never find a job that I love*, and this unconscious thought cancels out the positive with a negative charge.

It's about **noticing**. Becoming more in tune with your thoughts. It's not pushing the "bad" thought away; it's more about bringing a heightened awareness to what you are thinking and then learning how to reframe that negative concept with a positive affirmation and practicing it.

We are all made up of opposing traits. We laugh and cry. We are capable of love and hate. We make good and bad choices. When we learn to acknowledge the complementary opposites within, we become gentler with ourselves and create intimacy with our wholeness. There lies freedom.

Affirmation: Today, I am gentle with myself. I keep peace in my soul.

Your Language Will Shape Your Relationship with Your Soul

In this book, you will find fifty-two inspirations with accompanying affirmations. The ideas and affirmations in this book are presented simply and with brevity to help you discern what's important to you and form a commitment to yourself.

Because there are fifty-two inspirations, you might choose to focus on one for each week of the year. You can go through the book in order or choose topics based on what intuitively feels right to you. I hold the strong belief that we are all intuitive and can learn **how to develop a relationship with our soul.**

Begin your days by taking a quiet moment each morning to consider a single page. You may choose to work with the affirmation presented or use it as an inspirational springboard to form one of your own. Once you've got your affirmation, repeat it out loud to yourself several times. I encourage you to write your affirmation in a journal, to see it in your own handwriting, and record the date. This practice lets you keep a log of all your affirmations and shows you where you've been and where you are headed. Work with each affirmation until you feel ready to move on. There is no right or wrong amount of time. Trust your gut; you will know when it's time to work on a new one. Make this time sacred, and let this commitment guide your day.

A New Irresistible Vibration

You are learning how to redirect your energies. If you dedicate a small but powerful amount of time each day, old habits will fall away, replaced with new energies that honestly feel really good. Your new language will begin to emit an irresistible energetic broadcast that helps you align to your divinity (as well as like-minded people, places, and opportunities.) When you've figured out how to identify a new vibrational relationship from within, you will have learned how to speak from your soul and you will attract what you affirm. Your life will shift.

Your journey progresses one day at a time. Let's start now.

Affirmation: My soul holds the answers deep within. I wake up to my life's breathtaking wonder.

1

Affirm What Your Soul Knows As True

Ask yourself, "What would I like to change in my life?" Keep it simple, and form this thought into a short, positive statement. This is your affirmation—your soul knows it is true (even if you don't yet believe it). Write this new declaration onto paper to cement it in your mind, being sure to write it in the present tense as if it's already happened. It's mystic law: if you put enough focused energy and attention into this statement, it will eventually come to fruition.

Affirm

My soul holds answers deep within.
I am healthy and happy.

2

Nature Heals

One of the quickest, surest ways I know to get reconnected with my body and its natural ability to heal itself is to spend some time in nature. Go outside. Maybe it's just walking to your car at the end of the day and feeling the fresh air on your face, looking up at a blue sky—or the rain, or the snow, or the swirling clouds—and feeling magically connected to it all. The Earth creates a sense of balance and healing. Let nature do its work. Heal yourself.

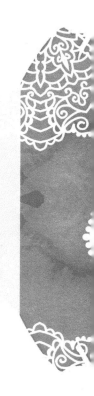

Affirm

*I spend time in nature and experience
healing and rejuvenation.*

3

Enlighten Up

Buddha said that if one human can become enlight-
ened, then everyone has the ability to attain this state.
Enlightenment does not mean being perfect. It means there
is no fight within. It means there is purity and clarity. Of
course, there will still be emotions of anger, frustration, or
worry, but the difference is that there is surrender to the
circumstance, and trust in the guidance of a divine hand
so that our pure energy—our Buddha nature—can shine
through.

Affirm

*I feel pure and full of energy
when there is no fight within.*

4

Take A Shower

Try this out. Next time you take your shower, be present in the shower. Notice wandering thoughts and each time bring your attention back to the experience of the shower. Feel the sensation of the cleansing water on your skin; allow the warmth of the water to relax your stiff muscles; become aware of the steamy air; smell the fresh scent of your shampoo as you massage your scalp; breathe in the aroma of your soap as it washes away the staleness of the previous day. Today, allow your awareness to be present in the shower.

Affirm

While I shower, I keep my attention on the experience of my shower. I step out refreshed, relaxed and ready to greet the day.

5

A New Perspective

Think for a moment about something or someone in your life that drives you crazy, something that really makes you nuts or gets right under your skin . . . have you got it? Know that this very issue, this annoyance or problem, is actually your ticket to a better life. It is in your life, "in your face," for a reason—to help you to discover, learn, and grow. Perhaps the biggest problem in your life right now is actually an opportunity just waiting to lead you to a new place.

Affirm

*I see my irritations as
opportunities to learn. I see my challenges
as leading me to a better place.*

6

Swim in Your Own Lane

In conversation with my good friend Hank, a former competitive swimmer and now a successful businessman in the health and wellness world, we discussed the motto his swimming coach taught him years ago. Swim in your own lane. This message is about paying attention to your own business (whether that's minding your own or running one) and not worrying about what others are doing around you. Yes, of course its okay to glance over, but don't lose time in really looking. Keep your focus on what you are doing.

Affirm

I swim in my own lane and I feel empowered.

7

Big Picture

Many times we think we know exactly what we want, and so we create affirmations that declare that very specific desire. Time and time again I have found that it's better to let the divine guide me along my path. Sometimes when we get too specific about our goals, we end up with just what we asked for—but something we discover we actually don't really want. When working with affirmations, keep your short positive statement broad but loaded with intention and desire. Let go of the details and look for the bigger picture.

Affirm

*I let go of the details and trust
in the bigger picture.*

8

The Greatest Instrument
You'll Ever Own

Awaken the intelligence of your body. It innately fights off invaders, rebuilds, purifies, and produces elixirs of hormones capable of making us happy or creating a baby. Your body turns the air you breathe into the perfect amount of oxygen and gets rid of the unwanted carbon dioxide, it pumps purified blood to your organs, and the list goes on. Magically, the bulk of this all happens "behind the scenes," automatically. That's why you must honor your body and it's wisdom— when given half a chance, it knows exactly what to do.

Affirm

I am grateful for my body. I trust that my
body's internal matrix is magical and wise.

9

One Thing at a Time

Today, take notice when you are doing something that feels mundane, such as waiting in line, walking (even if it's to the bathroom), or listening to a boring conversation—something that seems like a complete waste of your time. Try this 3,000-year-old Zen mindfulness meditation practice: slow down and keep your attention in that "mundane" moment. Rather than succumbing to frustration or boredom, allow this time to be a reprieve. A beautiful way to be present and shift your feelings in your day.

Affirm

I use the power of my attention and
stay present with one thing at a time.

10

Patience As a Hard Discipline

It is not just waiting until something happens over which we have no control: the arrival of the bus, the end of the rain, the return of a friend, the resolution of a conflict. Patience is not waiting passively until someone else does something. Patience asks us to live the moment to the fullest, to be completely present to the moment, to taste the here and now, to be where we are. When we are impatient, we try to get away from where we are. We behave as if the real thing will happen tomorrow, later, and somewhere else. Be patient and trust that the treasure you are looking for is hidden in the ground on which you stand.

—Henri Nouwen

Affirm

*I am patient with myself and others.
I trust that my greatest treasures
are with me in every moment.*

11

Unplug Everyday

The first step to bringing a sense of calm into your everyday is keeping it all in balance. How wonderful to be tapped into a means of connecting with the wider world, but it's equally important to create sacred space. Unplug every day. Unplug from your phone, your computer, your television—everything. Just for 20 minutes. When you spend time in silence, you reconnect to who you are. And when you visit this place regularly, you make room in yourself to serve others better.

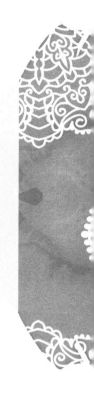

Affirm

*I will unplug for 20 minutes. I am
rejuvenated and refreshed.*

12

Live like a Yogi

Yoga, with its 5,000 years of wisdom, literally works like magic. At first, you just feel good from practicing the postures—so you keep doing them. But then something special begins to happen. The practice of yoga can be very simple, and yet in its simplicity it begins to create subtle shifts that somehow seep into your soul. The process wakes you up. You begin to recognize what is important in your every day and uncover a sense of purpose. You are inspired and guided to live the life you are meant to live. Yoga becomes part of your every day, a way of living with deepened awareness of what really matters. As this feeling grows, it takes on a life of its own and has very little to do with a physical practice on a mat. Although the physical practice is where it all begins. The increasing popularity of yoga is no secret; if there isn't a yoga studio near you, look to your nearest fitness center or download a video. It's all about trying different styles and teachers and discovering what style you enjoy. Just do it.

Affirm

*I commit to a daily yoga practice and
take ownership of my body and my life.*

13

The Golden Rule

The golden rule: Do unto others as you would do unto yourself. It is a message that withstands generations, holds the potential to unify political and religious borders, and is comprehended (though not always applied) by people aged 2 to 102 years old. As Atticus tells Scout in the classic novel *To Kill A Mockingbird*, "You never really understand a person until you consider things from his point of view . . . until you climb into his skin and walk around in it."

Affirm

I treat others as I would like to be treated.

14

Focus

I love to take photographs. I particularly like one style of shot, known as a "bokeh." This way of photographing obscures (or blurs out) everything in the background that is a distraction. The camera then sharply pulls into focus whatever you choose. The same concept works well in our day-to-day life. When we focus, the things that matter move to the forefront with crystal clarity and everything else fades away.

Affirm

My focused attention brings me clarity.

15

Meditate on That

Between them, Harvard, Princeton, Yale, and MIT have conducted more than 1,200 scientific studies that prove the numerous benefits of meditation—things like decreasing pain and inflammation and increasing positive emotions and life satisfaction. For me, meditation has been a daily discipline. It's worth every ounce of effort for the increased clarity, calm confidence, and heightened intuition it brings. Dedicate a small portion of your morning to find pure stillness, with no expectation—just the enjoyment of quiet space—everyday.

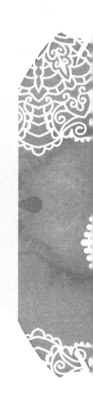

Affirm

I spend five minutes in meditation. In my
stillness, I am spontaneously healing.

16

Leave the Light On

I like to leave our porch light on in the evening hours, and sometimes even all night long. The light shining out through the darkness brings me comfort and a secure feeling. Do you leave a light on in your home? Consider that this light is just like the light deep within your soul. It is always on, always shining. Everything that happens in your day, positive and negative, creates an opportunity to bring you back home to yourself and to your light within. Let it connect you to a higher power, one that has unlimited potential.

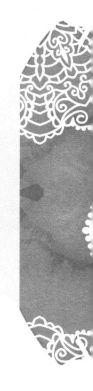

Affirm

*I use my everyday experiences to
connect me to the light that lives
inside me. I feel empowered.*

17

Your Sacred Space

A sacred space is not necessarily a place—it can be an action or activity in which you enjoy peacefulness and creativity. You can find this feeling, this "space," in exercising, walking in nature, working in your garden, or creating your art and craft. You can access it through prayer, meditation, or just the pure enjoyment of time alone. These are the moments when you rebirth and renew yourself into the next point in time. Honor your space in a sacred way, with purpose and intention.

Affirm

*I honor my sacred space. My ability to be
in relationships with others is expanded
because I allow myself solitude and creativity.*

18

Let Go of that Thought

When you fight with thoughts, they gain momentum. Is the cranky lunch waitress still in your thoughts later in the afternoon? Or is a morning conversation that went wrong on constant re-play in your mind? Repeated negative thoughts zap power just by getting you to engage with them. The minute you "let go," you can experience neutral space (a feeling free from good or bad, yes or no), and inner healing begins. In this space we feel lighter.

Affirm

*I notice my thoughts and let go of
those that don't serve me.*

19

Follow the Sun

The sun's warm and friendly energy heals body and soul. When skin is exposed to moderate amounts of sunshine, the body makes vitamin D, which helps absorb calcium and makes bones strong—and it does more than that, too. It also significantly improves your mood. Just think about how you feel on a cloudy gray day versus a sunny day. Sunshine is a gift from nature's soul energy, shining before us. And, if your current weather is gray and cloudy use this opportunity to visualize; recall a memory of a sunshine-filled day and soak in the feeling through the power of your imagination.

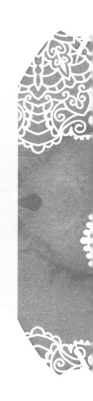

Affirm

*I step out and enjoy the sunshine. The
sun's warm energy brings me strength
and positive power for my day.*

20

Just Breathe

Whenever you feel stressed today take a few moments to stop and just be with your breath. Use this technique to soothe you right now: Bring all of your awareness to your body. Just think about what you can feel. Feel your feet touching the ground. Feel your bottom sitting in your chair, your head and neck in line with your spine. Now bring your attention to your breath. Notice that you are breathing. Feel your breath moving in and out more strongly. INHALE. EXHALE. Notice how your breath begins to make space in your body and creates more space between your thoughts.

Affirm

I use my breath as a tool and
I am calm and centered.

21

Happiness

It's not always easy to feel happy. Through my yoga education my swami taught me something that I continue to practice today. She said, "first thing when you wake up in the morning, before you get out of bed, ask yourself, am I happy?" This sounds a simple thing to do, but watch how it packs a powerful punch. Somewhere between sleep and wake we become more honest with ourselves. Try it. Being authentic with yourself will guide you along your path to freedom, joy, and happiness.

Affirm

*Upon waking, I ask myself, am I
happy? I listen to the answer and
act on my revealed feelings.*

22

Ready, Set, Goal

When you are in your quiet space, use this beautiful time to turn inward and reflect on where you put your energies. Take a pen to paper and write down the top three places you put your energy. Can you look back and feel good about where you are investing your time? Are your actions aligning with your goals? If not, what would you change? Now write one place you aspire to invest your energy.

Affirm

*My actions align with my goals
and create my life.*

23

Forgive

Holding on to anger is like grasping a hot coal; you are the one that gets burned.

—Buddha

This quote reminds me how I shackle myself in my own misery when I do not forgive. The very moment I let go, there is new space for a lightness that opens my heart. This is when healing begins.

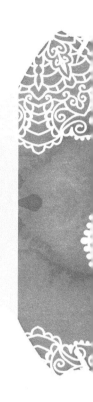

Affirm

*Every day I see things (big and small) that I
can forgive and I feel the freedom in forgiving.*

24

Life Brings Us Signposts

Have you ever noticed a serendipitous moment? The same song plays on the radio, in the elevator, and then later in the grocery store? What are the lyrics—is this an important message for you? Maybe a butterfly lands next to you and its beautiful presence makes you feel connected to your spirit, or you coincidently run into an old friend after just thinking of them. What does it mean? Be open to the possibility that a signpost may be planted right next to you. How many have you let slip away?

Affirm

*I notice serendipitous events and
I listen to the message.*

25

Make the Time, Find the Time

My daughter Allie and I were discussing the personal discipline of our daily yoga practice. She likes to attend group classes and I prefer to practice on my mat at home. We also talked about how at first you "find the time" to practice, and then once you come to understand the benefits of a daily discipline, you make the time. Just like you make the time to wash your face and brush your teeth every morning. It's a necessary part of your day. Make the time.

Affirm

I make the time to take care of me today.

26

Baby, Go Relax

Relaxed and calm, your body is closer to its true natural state and is able to heal and renew. Try this simple technique: Completely relax for five minutes in the morning before you get out of bed, and five minutes in the evening before you go to sleep. This means lying still with your eyes closed (lightly awake), focusing on your breath and relaxing each part of your body with the help of your breath. Most importantly, notice how you feel after you relax. Soon your body will crave this feeling, and your practice will become a welcomed if not essential part of your day.

Affirm

I relax and allow my body to self-heal.

27

Uncover the Goodness Within

When Michelangelo carved the David out of marble, he said the statue was always there; he just needed to be uncovered. When we pay attention to this powerful message, we begin to understand who we are, and what we need to do in our daily existence. Each of us has something to give, something beautiful within us that perhaps just needs to be uncovered. Our gifts are greater than we think. When we are in the flow, we uncover our true potential and our actions are fueled with love and filled with joy. Giving to others is a gift we give ourselves.

Affirm

*I uncover my own goodness and others share
in the benefits of the best version of me.*

28

Ten Years From Now

I love to visualize. It's been a long-time practice for myself to visualize life in the future, and when teaching others I often use this same technique. We look to the future, whether it's one, five, or ten years down the road. Visualizations are not only fun, they are also a great way to relax into yourself and your future. Spend a little time in the playground of your imagination and visualize yourself in ten years. If you have a little more time, write it down. You may be surprised with your results. Think big.

Affirm

I use my imagination as a playground.
I visualize my best self.

29

Read Between the Lines

Today, adjust your focus and allow yourself to see things that aren't visible and hear things that are unspoken. Learn to "read between the lines," and your perception shifts. When you see with compassionate eyes and listen with an open heart you feel less tense and more at ease. The way you respond to your environment changes. Try it now. Allow this new way of seeing and feeling to take you by the hand and lead you to a healthier, happier, more peaceful way.

Affirm

*I see with compassionate eyes
and hear with an open heart.*

30

Heaven on Earth

Have you ever caught yourself saying this is just heaven on Earth? Perhaps you experience this when you feel love deeply, appreciate real beauty, truly taste food, or feel immense gratitude. Take a moment to remember how this special sensation feels and allow this awareness to infuse into your day. Find the things in your day that bring you to this place.

Affirm

*I allow the feeling of 'heaven on
earth' to weave into my day.*

31

Nine

Tap into the number nine. Through my yoga education I learned to connect with my breath and count backward from nine (as a way to occupy my mind and therefore still my thoughts). Try it for yourself and use the number nine today. Place your hand on your abdomen, and feel your breath naturally deepen into your belly. Belly breathing is a beautiful way to relax your body and mind. Notice your hand moving in and out as you breath deeply; now count your breaths backward from nine.

Affirm

*I practice belly breathing, and
tap into the power of nine.*

32

Bloom, Little Flower

There is a crack in everything. That's what lets the light shine in.

—Leonard Cohen

Think of a daisy as it pushes its way up through a crack in the cement. This flower's power comes from its deeply grounded roots. As the bloom moves toward the light it finds freedom and growth. In your most authentic self, there will always be imperfections, but when you honor your whole self, (the good and the shadow) these parts of us let our beauty shine straight through.

Affirm

*I am my authentic self and feel
my light shine from inside out.*

33

The Shadow,
Embracing Wholeness

To work on our light, we also have to journey into the shadow. Affirmations ask us to look at our "shadow" side—to understand our own negative and positive qualities. When we own up to our own traits and are honest about them to ourselves, we move into a place of true compassion and understanding of ourselves and others. In our humility, we come into power.

Affirm

I accept myself for all that I am.
In my humility I feel powerful.

34

Feel Peace

Just for a moment, instead of a tornado of responsibilities, stress, and mayhem, imagine a deliciously calm sense of quiet. A space of serene tranquility. A mind at peace. Stillness. Freedom. Strength. This is a moment's peace, and it can be yours everyday. What does a moment's peace feel like to you?

Affirm

*Anytime I feel stress today, I notice
my reaction to this feeling—I pause,
and let go. I am at peace.*

35

Sixth Sense

Everyone has intuition. Everybody. Intuition boils down to paying attention. Through daily practice and focused attention, we begin to become accustomed to our gut feelings. Tapping into this sixth sense begins with heightening your other five. What does it feel like to be more aware of all of your senses? Today, give more attention to smells, sights, sounds, tastes, and the feeling of the world around you. As you hone in on your five, the sixth (your intuition) comes more into play.

Affirm

I tap into all of my senses and "feel" my way through my day.

36

Be Gentle On Yourself

Be gentle with yourself. You are a child of the universe, no less than the trees and the stars. In the noisy confusion of life, keep peace in your soul.

—Max Ehrman

Some days it's hard to be gentle on yourself. It's a practice.

Affirm

I am gentle with myself. I keep peace in my soul.

37

Abundance

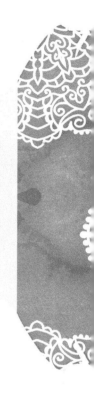

On a retreat in Mexico, we had the opportunity to do a special ritual with a native shaman. He asked us to sit in a circle and in turn go around the circle and give a word or feeling (that we felt we held in abundance) to the person next to us. Things like love, peace, kindness, and magic. Try this for yourself. Tune into the vibration of abundance. From your heart center, feel abundance trickle through you. Now share this abundant feeling with someone. The point is, when you visualize that your abundant feeling is in surplus, you have so much abundance that you have more than enough and that makes you want to share it even more. It's a sense of generosity and gratitude overflowing.

Affirm

*I feel abundant. In my generosity,
I am abundant.*

38

Shine Bright

My friend Dawn had a lifetime career as a hairdresser, but was tired of working for others and sick of the pettiness and gossip hives of salons. She was ready for a big shift; she knew something needed to change. She focused clearly on her desire for a big change. Next she formed her resolve into a positive statement for change, creating a powerful affirmation: "I shine throughout my day, I am filled with abundance and time for family." Keeping her affirmation broad but loaded with intention and desire, she let go of the details and held onto the bigger picture. She got out of her own way and let her soul guide her. Within a month or so the opportunity arose for her to open her own salon. This new venture meant taking a big risk. She kept the faith and took the leap. She and her family now own a beautiful light-filled space with the intention (written on the wall) to make women feel beautiful from the inside out. They named their new salon, SHINE.

Affirm

*I shine throughout my day, I am filled
with abundance and time for family.*

39

Relaxation in a Nutshell

Do you feel there is never enough time in the day to dedicate to the indulgence of relaxation? What if I showed you a way? Practicing mindful breathing and body awareness are things you can do anywhere, anytime—in your home, on a bus, in an airplane, at a desk, or waiting for your turn in line. Every day, spend some time focusing on your breath and concentrating on your body and your body will respond in a beautiful way. As you begin, stay focused on each part of your body. As soon as you notice your attention becoming distracted and moving elsewhere, gently and firmly bring it back to your body and your breath.

Affirm

*I practice breathing and body
awareness. I am relaxed.*

40

Be Mindful of What You Wish For

My daughter Sarah arrived home after attending a summer course in London. She was happy to see all of us, but the first thing she declared was "I am going back." We laughed at her directness, but we also recognized that she was listening to her heart (and soul). Her dad said, "Go to London, but know that you are going to have to find a job there to cover the high cost of living." Sarah contacted everyone she could think of. Every morning she woke up with a strong intention and the affirmation, I have a job in London that only I can do, I am a talented soul and I feel freedom and joy in what I do. After some worrying, she realized she needed to let go, stay positive, and be grateful for her current life. That is when the magic happened. Her job offer arrived. Sarah moved to London for a period and is thrilled to remind us, "be mindful of what you wish for."

Affirm

*I choose my thoughts and affirmations
carefully, as they become my reality.*

41

Let's Dance

Yogi Bhajan said, "you have thirty trillion cells and God is dancing with them—and you are part of that dance."

When you trust that the divine lives within, you surrender to its rhythms. You trust that everything is just as it should be and your life flows like an effortless dance.

Affirm

*I feel the dance of light within every cell
of my body and I trust it's rhythm.*

42

That's Good Enough

If you strive to treat everyone with respect, work hard, be the person that is willing to help, and practice humility, you are doing your best. Also if you stand up to the people and the situations in life that will challenge you to go against these values—you have done your best. And, that is good enough.

Affirm

I do my best and that is good enough.

43

Your Body is a Reservoir

Your body is just like a reservoir. Everyday, life presents you with a myriad of physical and emotional experiences that slowly and surely take up most of the room in your reservoir. Too many stressors and claims to your attention add up to physical and emotional exhaustion; your reservoir becomes filled to the brim, overflows, and causes the dam to break. Make space within your personal reservoir by intentionally creating ways to de-stress and take a step back from day-to-day busy-ness. This allows you the capacity to be healthy and happy, so that even in the midst of a stress-filled day you have some extra room to maneuver.

Affirm

*I notice how full my reservoir
feels. I take time to de-stress.*

44

Present Moment, Beautiful Moment

What are some of the ways you spend time during your day? Sitting in traffic. Waiting for your dinner to cook. Running a meeting. Folding laundry. Showering. Dressing. Life might find you doing any of these activities. In fact, chances are you often do more than one of them at the same time, hurrying, rushing. When you bring your awareness to the task at hand, you exist in the present moment. You allow yourself to feel the beauty of this moment and feel relaxed and energized.

Affirm

*I focus my awareness on the task at hand
and I feel the beauty of this moment.*

45

What Do You Love To Do?

What do you love to do? What do you do love to do so much that you lose track of time doing it? Finish this sentence; I love to . . . And then answer: how do I feel when I am doing this thing? Whatever the activity may be—cooking, exercising, laughing, hugging—these actions are you in a joyful expression. These actions let you feel how good it is to be in a true expression of yourself. Do you make time to do the things you love to do?

Affirm

I spend time doing something I love to do.

46

Good Vibes Only

How do you attract good, positive vibrations into your life? By being a positive vibration yourself. I even made *Good Vibes* my car's license plate as a reminder. Today create good vibes for someone else. Do something kind. Give someone a compliment in their day. Everyone has something good and beautiful about them that they're waiting to hear. When we send out good vibes, it's a direct line to receiving a good feeling back, creating your own good vibration.

Affirm

*I feel good vibrations and I
send out good vibrations.*

47

Visualize This

Creative visualization can take many forms, and it's a technique I practice and teach often. I find that when it comes down to our core values; love, gratitude, and peace are often the essence of what we truly want. Other things take a back seat. Take a moment and indulge yourself in the luxury of visualization. Settle into your body through a few deep and relaxed breaths. Now imagine yourself surrounded by love and filled with gratitude and deep peace. Will you let yourself have a life filled with these virtues?

Affirm

My life is filled with love, gratitude,
and peace, and I feel it.

48

Light Me Up

It took me many years to finally get this lesson, but I feel I have finally become wise enough to discern for myself who I want to share my time with and who really matters to me. I have vowed to surround myself with people who embody love and light, and recognize that I am the only one who can be the judge of who brings me joy, light, and laughter.

Affirm

I notice how other people make me feel. I choose to be around people who lift me up.

49

Call in the Troops

I come as one, but I stand as 10,000.

—Paraphrased from the poem
"Our Grandmothers," by Maya Angelou

What a beautiful reminder, that we are never alone. Think of a time when you really needed some extra support. A time when you felt alone in your work, craft, or mission. Now imagine that as you stand before the meeting, the project, the conversation, you come as one, but you stand with the support of generations of ancestors who came before you. Grandmothers and their grandmothers who believe in the very essence of you and what you are doing. Imagine that they are standing with you, watching over you, cheering you on, emboldening you with determination and filling you up with gumption.

Affirm

I call on my ancestors and I feel their support.

50

Serenity Prayer

God, grant me the serenity to accept the things I cannot change, courage to change the things I can, and wisdom to know the difference.

—Unknown

Who doesn't get caught up in the wear and tear of everyday life? How often do we forget to take a step back and look at the bigger picture? Whenever we feel confused, frustrated, or angry, we often try to find somewhere else to put the blame. What if instead of passing the buck we thought to ourselves: "there is no need for blame." **Grant me the serenity to accept the things I cannot change.** What can we change? We can choose to invest our energy in the positive—people, places, and things. Spend time with those who uplift and support you, be in places that "just feel good," and give your attention to where you put your energy. **Grant me the courage to change the things I can.** How easy it is to get the two ideas confused. **Grant me the wisdom to know the difference.**

Affirm

*I accept the things I cannot change, have
the courage to change the things I can, and
find the wisdom to know the difference.*

51

Dream On

For years our family has shared our nighttime (and future) dreams. When we are all together, breakfast conversation is most often about someone's dream the night before. Whether the dream is in a code or quite literal, they always hold a message. Dreams are typically about ourselves, and who better to share them with than the people who know and love you the most? In our house, we help each other work through the previous night's messages and relish in their ability to uncover a hidden truth. If you honor your dream world and pay attention to your dreams, they will reveal uncanny, important messages. Your dreams are a beautiful way to find out what is going on in your subconscious mind. Think of it this way: your nighttime inner-self is trying to get a message to your daytime outer-self.

Affirm

I pay attention to my dreams and
they bring me messages.

52

Speak Soul Language

Your soul holds the answers. Take a moment to become quiet and still. Ask yourself, "What more would I like to change in my life?" This is not a wish or a hope, it's a positive resolve for change. Form this affirmation into the present tense and repeat it to yourself. You have learned how to develop a relationship with your soul and how to speak soul language. You hold the power to step forward into your beautiful life, the one that has always been there, waiting for you.

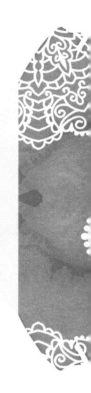

Affirm

*I hold deep inner wisdom and
I speak from my soul.*

About the Author

Elizabeth Irvine is a nurse, educator, and award-winning author. Her philosophy and teachings are based on thirty years' experience as a health care professional and her yogic style of living, both of which provide the foundation of her work today.

Irvine's previously published works, *Healthy Mother Healthy Child*, *A Moment's Peace*, and *Meditations from the Earth*, all provide a calming and healing influence along with simple steps to bring peace and serenity into the home.

Irvine contributes a monthly column for *Houston Family Magazine*, facilitates workshops, and leads retreats for intimate groups in locations around the world. A new focus of her work is one-to-one sessions and virtual workshops.

She invites you to join the Truewellbeing community and enlighten your inbox with her e-inspiration for a weekly dose of good vibes. Learn more and connect at www.truewellbeing.com.

CPSIA information can be obtained
at www.ICGtesting.com
Printed in the USA
BVHW021027050121
597030BV00021B/211/J